X

GREAT CRYSTAL BEAR

WRITTEN BY **Carolyn Lesser**   ILLUSTRATED BY **William Noonan**

HARCOURT BRACE & COMPANY   San Diego   New York   London

Text copyright © 1996 by Carolyn Lesser
Illustrations copyright © 1996 by William Noonan

Requests for permission to make copies of any part of the work should
be mailed to: Permissions Department, Harcourt Brace & Company,
6277 Sea Harbor Drive, Orlando, Florida 32887-6777.

Library of Congress Cataloging-in-Publication Data
Lesser, Carolyn.
Great crystal bear/Carolyn Lesser; illustrated by William Noonan.—1st ed.
p.   cm.
Summary: A great polar bear sleeps, hunts, wanders, and mates as the seasons pass.
ISBN 0-15-200667-2
1. Polar bear—Juvenile fiction. [1. Polar bear—Fiction. 2. Bears—Fiction.]
I. Noonan, William, 1923-   ill. II. Title.
PZ10.3.L553Gr 1996
[E]—dc20 95-12383

First edition   A B C D E

Printed in Singapore

With love, I thank my father, Karl Schmidt, who many years ago

wrapped me in a blanket and carried me into a snowy Wisconsin

night, saying, "Look . . . the aurora borealis."

For expertise, encouragement, and friendship,

I thank Dan Guravich, Ph.D., Nikita Ovsyanikov, Ph.D.,

and Jo Dwyer.   —C. L.

The illustrations in this book were done in watercolor

and water-soluble dyes on watercolor paper.

The display and text type were set in Bernhard Gothic.

Color separations by Bright Arts, Ltd., Singapore

Printed and bound by Tien Wah Press, Singapore

This book was printed with soya-based inks on Leykam recycled

paper, which contains more than 20 percent postconsumer

waste and has a total recycled content of at least 50 percent.

Production supervision by Warren Wallerstein and Ginger Boyer

Designed by Camilla Filancia

For Bill Wesp and the light-spirits, who know

—C. L.

For my daughter, Barbara Holland

—W. N.

Great crystal bear,

Alone

In the vast winter darkness,

Are you the mystical Nanuk of Inuit legend,

A man who enters an igloo

And emerges a bear, dressed in fur?

Perhaps you are the magical bear

Helping the shaman consult with spirits.

The Lapps called you "God's dog,"

"The old man in the fur cloak,"

Afraid to offend you by saying "bear."

"Twelve men's strength and eleven men's wit,"

Norse songs sang of you,

Revered king of the Arctic.

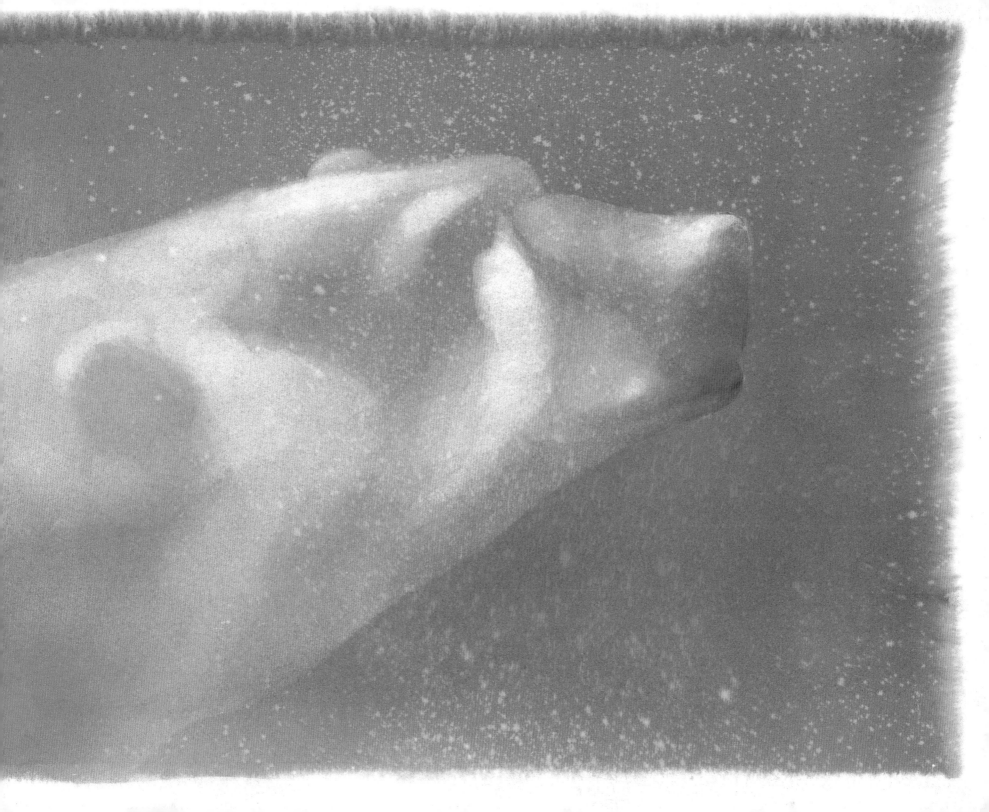

Great crystal bear,

How do you survive on the thick ice

Covering the deep Arctic sea?

As you pad through the storm wind,

Veils of snow race past your fringy paws.

Time to scoop a hollow in a drift

And huddle in,

Back to the wind,

Nose pushed under the snow,

Paws snuggling your body.

Winds howl. Snow swirls,

Covering you like dust until you vanish.

Sleep warm, crystal bear.

The earth leans far from the sun

As you rouse from your drift-bed

This winter solstice morning.

How lucky that every other day of the year

Each hollow hair of your fur

Gathers sunlight

To heat your black skin and thick layer of fat.

Your blubbery blanket keeps you warm

For long, dog-paddling swims

And months of day-and-night

Winter wandering.

As you wander, great bear,

Your keen nose smells

Bear friends and relatives nearby.

Some nap behind hills of ice.

Others travel.

They are like you,

Comforted by the scent of companions

But on singular journeys,

Alone, but not lonely.

Carefully climbing a mountain
Of wind-piled pack ice,
Your hind feet step neatly into footprints
Made by your front paws.
You stand on top, stretching twelve feet tall,
Sniffing the air and the Arctic sea.
Seals are near.

You clamber down
And rush toward the scent,
Pacing over smooth ice
On gritty paws that never slip.
As you near a snow-covered mound,
Your footfalls slow,
Silenced by fur between your paw pads.
Flopping on your belly,
You glide downwind of the dome
Over the seal's breathing hole.
Pushing with hind legs,
Pulling with front claws,
You inch closer . . . closer . . . stop.
Silent as light, still as fallen snow,
You wait all day for a seal to breathe.

Great crystal bear,
You have fooled the seal
Swimming under you.
He surfaces and gulps for air.
Your paws, heavy as sledgehammers,
Smash the ice dome.
Your mouth grabs the seal, jerks it up, out.
You feast for hours on skin and blubber,
Stopping often for a snow bath.
Finished, you nap. The carcass waits
For those who follow in twilight or darkness.
Mothers with cubs, young bears, and foxes
Need the meat you leave.
They depend on your planning and power.

Great crystal bear, trotting alone,

What calls you to journey

Far across boundless ice?

Mighty northwest winds cause ice to drift east,

Pile high, and collapse.

Landmarks are everchanging.

What sense tells you to wander west,

Tells you where your boundaries are?

And when you find a female's scent,

Nothing will stop your race to her.

You cross ice and open ocean

In a straight line.

You travel as far as you must,

Battle if you must, to mate with her.

Then you go on, never knowing the cubs

She brings from her den

Into spring sunshine.

Perhaps one will grow to be like you,

Great bear.

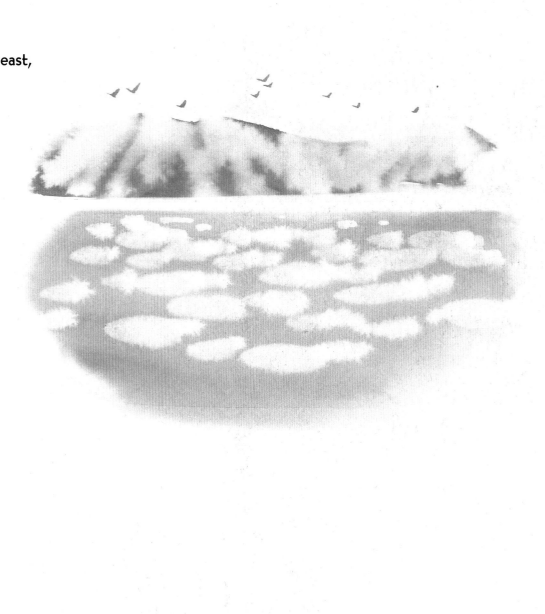

Great crystal bear,

In a golden sunrise

The snow goose and gander huddle on their nest,

Spring-gale snow piling to their heads.

Fat from winter kills,

You waddle past their peering eyes,

Leaving wide tracks.

You follow retreating sea ice into deep bays,

Stride over softening ice like a skater,

Sprawl as it bends under your weight.

Each day the sun rises higher,

Carving solid ice into islands.

You leap from one floe to another,

Swim farther, longer.

When you are overheated and tired,

You haul out, shake dry,

And nap on an ice pillow, drifting for miles.

Suddenly you wake, sniff, stand, look.

A seal sleeps on the edge of the ice,

Looks up, and sleeps again.

You slip into the water, feet first,

As if poured into the sea.

Stalking, you hang motionless as an ice floe,

Only eyes, nose, and ears above water,

Front paws paddling, back paws steering.

Then, without sound or splash,

You slink under water, under ice.

Webbed paws big as plates pull strong,

Take you deep into forests of kelp

That hide starfish and shrimp, worms and anemones.

Whoosh! You rocket from the sea

And strike the seal dead in one blow, one bite.

You hunt tirelessly every spring day to store fat.

Seals are scarce. Winds are warming.

One day ice islands soften, sag,

Surrender to seawater.

Great crystal bear,

Summer light casts long shadows.

Ice and seals are gone.

You come ashore to wander the capes

And headlands in cool offshore breezes.

You follow tracks to other bears.

All nod friendliness, circle, nuzzle muzzles.

A young male challenges you to wrestle,

Then another and another.

You play-fight with one at a time,

Never growling or biting hard.

They learn to fight for a mate,

To fight only when necessary,

For in the Arctic

Severe injury means certain death.

After the lesson, hot and exhausted,

You flop with the young bears

On the cool gravel beach and nap.

Great crystal bear,

The summer sun is a powerful enemy,

More powerful than the icy winter wind.

Your stored fat must keep you alive.

Some days you search for berries,

Nibble sparse grasses and kelp,

Try to catch an elusive squirrel or lemming

Or an eider duck swimming in the bay.

To cool off you pant and sprawl and swim

Or roll over, waving your legs in the breeze

So heat will escape from your foot pads.

You excavate a bed on the permafrost,

Hidden in a thicket of willows.

Protected from the sun, you sleep.

Life happens in slow motion, in walking hibernation.

It is time to watch and wait.

Great crystal bear,

As the days pass you amble along the beach,

Sniffing, watching, listening.

The sea and air tell you fall is coming.

Daylight hours are shorter.

Swans take flight. Snow falls.

Your tracks are narrow, thin bear.

Each morning you pace faster,

Looking, sniffing the sea.

The air is cold.

An oily crust of ice

Forms on the still water of tidal ponds.

Every day is colder, the wind bolder.

Fierce winds crush ice crystals,

Whipping them into a thick soup.

Snow and slush freeze together.

Chunks and clumps collide.

The ice is alive.

Listen. What does it tell you?

Bays fill with sheets of ice.

Rocked by tides and currents, they break

And float like gigantic frozen lily pads.

Eager to hunt, you step on them, crash through.

Perhaps tomorrow, great bear.

Great crystal bear,

As you awaken this day,

Mist clouds the air.

Sea smells call you back to your native ice.

Tides and currents and winds lift, push, pull.

Ice grinds, booms, cracks.

Snow squalls blur land and sky.

Arctic gale winds ruffle your fur.

Gingerly you test the ice again.

Each step sounds like one long beat

On a high-pitched kettledrum.

The sea ice holds. Freeze-up has come at last.

On a head-swinging dead run,

You rush to meet your endless kingdom of drifting ice.

Winter is here.

Great crystal bear,

Alone

In the vast Arctic night,

Are you ready for your journey?

Clouds sail clear of the moon

And swirls of snow glow on the ice

As you pace through pools of moonlight.

The waving curtains of light are beckoning,

Weaving ribbons of color through stars.

The aurora borealis is your companion this night.

Some say the lights are the spirits of the old ones,

The ones who have gone before.

Their spirit-light will watch over you, the great Nanuk,

The one who is without shadow,

The mightiest of all.

Within you are the secrets of cold and alone.

Bon voyage, great crystal bear.